spend yourself rich!

A values-based approach to help you reach your financial dreams

by Grady Cash, CFP

FINANCIAL LITERACY CENTER
BUILDING TRUST THROUGH EDUCATION

Kalamazoo, Michigan

This publication is designed to provide authoritative information regarding the subject matter covered. The publisher is not engaged in rendering legal, accounting, or other professional services. If legal advice or other expert assistance is needed, the reader is advised to engage the services of a competent professional.

Published by the Financial Literacy Center
350 East Michigan Avenue
Kalamazoo, MI 49007-3851
(888) 679-3300

Publisher's Cataloging-in-Publication
(Provided by Quality Books, Inc.)

Cash, J. Grady, 1947–
    Spend yourself rich! : a values-based approach to help you reach your financial dreams / J.Grady Cash. -- 1st ed.
    p. cm.
    Includes bibliographical references (p.).
    LCCN: 97-61519
    ISBN 0-9659638-2-9

    1. Finance, Personal. 2. Self-realization. 3. Investments-- Moral and ethical aspects.   I. Title.

HG179.C37 1998   332.024
                         QBI97-1524

98765432
First Edition. Printed in the United States of America

For information on purchasing a copy of this book, please contact the Financial Literacy Center, 350 East Michigan Avenue, Kalamazoo, MI 49007-3851, or call (888) 679-3300.

Contents

Foreword

Spend Yourself Rich is an enticing promise — wouldn't we all like to spend our way to wealth? But Grady Cash isn't making an empty promise, or serving up a get-rich-quick scheme. In this book he does show all of us how we can spend ourselves rich, no matter what our income or circumstances.

Perhaps the most important contribution of this book, and what makes it stand apart from the many personal finance books already available, is the fact that Cash acknowledges we're all different when it comes to money. We have individual "spending personalities" that affect how we treat and use money. Whether you recognize yourself as an "impulsive spender," a "fanatical spender," or even a combination of Cash's seven spending personalities, you'll get helpful, smart, straightforward advice that can dramatically change your financial life.

Spend Yourself Rich starts in the right place — the heart. By reminding us that there are things money can and cannot buy, Cash encourages us to put our money where our values are, a proposition that's easy to lose sight of in our hectic day-to-day lives. By helping us focus first on our values, we can make much better decisions about how and where to spend our money. From there, Cash shows us how to save money, conquer debt, and trim expenses.

Listen to Grady Cash. He will show you how to spend yourself rich!

Gerri Detweiler
author, *The Ultimate Credit Handbook*

Acknowledgments

I'd like to thank those who helped make this book possible:

Dr. David Kentsmith, a clinical psychologist, who helped add depth to our early definitions of the spending personalities; kindred spirit Bob Czimbal, who edited the first draft; guardian angel Ahnna Lake, M.D., who edited an earlier version of this book, and my best friend and wife, Kathy, who helped in all stages of the book's development.

A special thanks to Christine Seibert for the major edit of this final text.

Finally, I'd like to thank Shawn Connors, whose vision and commitment made the publication of this work possible.

These kind souls, and other contributors too numerous to mention, have my lasting appreciation.

It is better to live rich than to die rich.

Samuel Johnson

Introduction

"Spend yourself rich! If all I had to do was spend money to be rich, I'd be a multimillionaire by now."

Impossible, you say? Perhaps, using traditional thinking about money. But that's what this book is about — developing a new attitude about money and a fresh perspective on managing it.

Money triggers more emotions than just about anything else in society today. It can give us our highest highs and our lowest lows. In fact, 40 percent of Americans think about money more often than they think about sex, according to "The Personality Factor: A *Worth*/Roper Survey of America's Inner Financial Life."

Yet, with all this interest in money, it's something we just don't like to talk about. We don't discuss our earnings in front of the kids for fear they'll share the information outside the home. We don't particularly like others to know what we paid for our homes and cars, or how much we have in savings or investments. The *Worth*/Roper survey mentioned above also found that of eight touchy subjects (including religion and politics), money was the one Americans feel the least comfortable discussing.

Perhaps that's why so many books have been written about the subject. If we can't talk about it openly, we'll learn through reading. Most written materials focus on two basic forms of money management: spending and saving. In *Spend Yourself Rich*, I'll simplify things even further by showing you how all the decisions you make about money (including saving and investing) are really spending decisions.

You'll find that your financial status is determined not by how much you earn or accumulate, but rather by how you spend what you have. As Paul Richard, educational director of the National Center for Financial Education, explains, "Everyday spending decisions have a far greater negative impact on your financial future than any investment decision you'll ever make. On average, Americans waste 10 to 20 percent of their income just through poor spending habits."

I'll also show you how your particular spending personality may be causing you to make spending mistakes that could keep you from reaching your goals. Of course, that assumes you have goals! You would be amazed at how many people do not have financial priorities. They honestly don't know what they want their money to do for them (other than getting them through the monthly bills). Setting goals, and learning to understand how your spending decisions affect those goals, is another valuable lesson this book provides.

First, however, a little background is in order. As a financial planner and investment advisor, I've managed money for some very successful, high-income individuals as well as many middle-income families. Eventually, my early training as a behavioral counselor led me to realize that I was not addressing the true needs of my clients.

Regardless of their incomes, they all needed more than traditional financial planning. They needed a better way to view money as part of their lives. This book will provide that new perspective — a simplified, values-based approach to personal finance.

Values-based personal finance

You'll discover how to make spending decisions based on your deeply felt values about life. This powerful technique cuts through the frustration and confusion so many people have with traditional money management.

According to Benjamin Franklin, "The use of money is all the advantage there is in having it." But it's *how* you use it that determines whether it brings you fulfillment. Knowing what you want your money to do for you — setting goals — is the first step toward making you a master of, and not a slave to, your money.

This is also one of the longest-lasting lessons you can teach your children. Kids always learn more from what we do than what we say. They learn to manage money from our example. I'll help you discover how to set and reach financial goals so you can pass the skills along to your children. Remember, you can teach them healthy or unhealthy money habits, just as you do with eating habits. It's a lesson money can't buy.

Four things money can buy

We know there are things money can't buy. But did you know that everything money *can* buy falls into only four categories? Most people spend their money in one category, when what they really want is in an entirely different category. Spending in the proper category to get what you really want could be *the most important financial lesson you'll ever learn.*

Money-saving tips

Don't worry, the book isn't all philosophy. It offers plenty of money-saving ideas you can put to work right away. For example, you'll learn tips to reduce debt and manage credit cards, and how to cut costs on everything from clothes and household expenses to driving. And, when you understand how to spend based on your personal values, you'll get the greatest benefit and enjoyment possible from every dollar you earn.

How to identify your spending personality

Most importantly, you will learn how to recognize your own subconscious spending personality, a pattern of spending habits that could sabotage your efforts to control your money. All of us make spending mistakes (money experts included!), but they result from very different habits and attitudes toward money. After taking the brief spending personality tests, you'll know which one of the seven personalities dominates your spending habits. And, as always, knowledge is power. Once you've learned to recognize the patterns, avoiding them becomes easier. Then you're on your way toward reaching the goals you have set for yourself.

Money will buy . . .
A bed, but not sleep;
A book, but not brains;
Food, but not an appetite;
Medicine, but not health;
Luxuries, but not culture;
Amusement, but not happiness.

Unknown

CHAPTER 1

Values-Based Money Management

A re you living in harmony with your personal values? Most of us would agree that we are. At the same time, most of us would also agree that it is difficult to define those very values that guide us through life.

Webster's dictionary describes a value as "that which is desirable or worthy of esteem for its own sake." And so, for the purpose of this book, we'll say that your values include the principles by which you live your life and those aspects of your life that carry long-term importance to you.

Yet, have you ever stopped to consider whether you're actually spending your money in a way that supports those values? You may think so, but my experience as a financial counselor raises doubts. Over the years, people have shared with me their goals and dreams, but when I looked at their financial statements, there was little indication that their spending was in harmony with those dreams.

Why? You might think it's because they don't have enough money to achieve what they desire. In some cases this is true, but more often than not, it's because they are misdirecting their financial resources to other areas. As a result, their spending habits may actually sabotage their chances of achieving their dreams.

In order to spend in harmony with your deeply felt values, you must first know what your values are and relate them to your goals. For example, if you value education, your goal may be to send your children to college. Or, if you place high value on a particular cause (e.g., child welfare, animal welfare, health, environment), your goal could be to support that cause financially or with time and energy.

What do most Americans value? The "Quality Quotient Survey," conducted by Bozell Worldwide found the following values listed as top priorities in life:

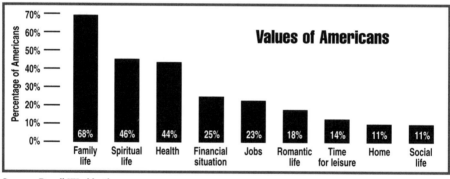

Source: Bozell Worldwide

Each of these values can support any number of different goals. "Financial situation," for example, could have any of the following as related goals:

- Retrain to improve your job skills.
- Plan for retirement.
- Plan for college education for the children.
- Pay off outstanding loans or bills.

Take college education. It's a common goal, but many people feel they don't have enough money to set aside to help their kids. Is this the case, or have they simply fallen into spending habits that don't support their goal?

The Life's Accomplishments worksheet on the next page will help determine your own deeply felt values. First, imagine that you are 20 years in the future and looking back on your life. What do you want to have

SPEND YOURSELF RICH

accomplished? Make a list of those accomplishments and circle the ones that you would be proudest of and cherish the most.

Next, move five years into the future and repeat the exercise. Finally, assume that you were to die six months from now. List what you would really want to accomplish in those six months, and circle those most important to you.

Life's Accomplishments

20 Years From Now	5 Years From Now	6 Months From Now
1 _____	1 _____	1 _____
_____	_____	_____
2 _____	2 _____	2 _____
_____	_____	_____
3 _____	3 _____	3 _____
_____	_____	_____
4 _____	4 _____	4 _____
_____	_____	_____
5 _____	5 _____	5 _____
_____	_____	_____

Now, look at your completed worksheet and decide if you are spending your money in a way that is helping you accomplish what you *really* want. If not, where can you spend less? Where should you spend more? Consider your time and energy, as well as your money, since these resources are also vital in achieving your dreams.

It All Comes Down to Spending

You've probably noticed that, so far, this book has said relatively little about saving. It's certainly not because saving is unimportant. Quite the contrary! But the fact of the matter is that all decisions regarding money are really spending decisions. Look at it this way: *Spending is simply a decision about when, where, and how to allocate your financial resources.* You might decide to allocate funds for investments, college, retirement, housing, transportation, entertainment, travel — the possibilities are endless.

Your financial status is determined more by what and how you *spend* than by what and how you *save*. Without control of your spending habits there will be little, if anything, left for saving!

Most people would be amazed to find out just how much discretionary income they really have. An analysis by TGE Demographics, Inc., published in *The Official Guide to American Incomes*, found that two-thirds of all households have some discretionary income — money they can spend on nonessentials. Of those households, the average amount was $13,480 in 1994. Surprised? That's because, like most of us, you probably can't account for where and how you spend much of your money.

In spite of that rather sizable amount, nearly half of us feel we're not faring as well as we expected to be doing five years ago, according to the 1995 "Americans and Their Money: The 10th National Survey" from *Money* magazine. The survey said more than half of us often worry about money, with the top concerns (in order): medical costs, retirement, education/college, food, housing, family member losing a job, and losing our own job.

All of these could be considered financial security issues. Yet even more important is your financial well-being — your attitude toward money and the role it plays in your life. Regardless of whether you struggle from paycheck to paycheck or have great wealth, you must address your attitude toward money if you ever hope to gain control over your finances.

Much of our self-image is wrapped up in the amount of money we make or the possessions we own. We attempt to measure our success with new cars and bigger homes. Too often, we think that how we spend our money demonstrates our achievements to others. In the end, our money is spent in the wrong places, and we're left feeling as though our true goals are out of reach. Sound familiar?

Perhaps an attitude adjustment is in order. It may not be more money that you need, but rather a realignment of your spending priorities. You may be pleasantly surprised to realize that you can reach many of your goals with a little planning.

But first, let's look at five basic truths about money.

1. **Money is not evil.** Money itself is just a resource. More money can give you greater freedom and independence. It can even provide the ability to help others less fortunate. It's perfectly acceptable to want to

SPEND YOURSELF RICH

make more money. Only when money is accumulated for its own sake, or its accumulation hurts others, does money create problems.

2. **Perceived needs expand with income.** As income increases, so does the perception of basic needs. These new perceived needs are really *"thinkwees"* — those items we *think we* need. Unless you make a conscious effort to avoid increased spending, every raise, every bonus, every income tax refund will be wasted on thinkwees.

3. **Your financial well-being is your responsibility.** You have no inherent right to money or success — only the right to *pursue* it. Whether you make it is up to you. You cannot delegate this responsibility to anyone else.

4. **You have been "programmed" to make spending mistakes.** Advertisers spend billions to convince consumers to buy their products, promising that you will look better, feel better, and be more successful. Even if you aren't directly influenced by this deluge of advertising, millions of your peers are. This creates a subtle, but powerful, peer pressure to buy what society expects you to buy. You can break this drain on your financial resources by recognizing the pressure for what it is, and making certain that you spend to reach *your* goals, not someone else's.

5. **Money can't buy happiness.** Money is not the best answer to many financial problems. But don't let the old "money can't buy happiness" cliché keep you from striving for financial well-being.

You may find some of these statements difficult to accept. Remember, they aren't necessarily fair, nor the way things *should* be. They are just the way life *is*. Accepting these truths can either be very constraining or very empowering, depending upon your perspective. *If you choose to see them as limiting, they most definitely will be limiting. If you choose to see them as saying your future is your responsibility, it is very empowering.* The choice is yours.

The Four Things Money Can Buy

As I noted earlier, most people are not reaching their goals and dreams because they are spending what they have in the wrong areas. Let's look at what money really can buy.

Possessions

Possessions are tangible items like cars, clothes, homes, and food. You certainly need shelter, food, and transportation, but do you really need a *new* car or those *new* clothes? These purchases may be "thinkwees" — you remember, those unnecessary things we think we need. Society, advertising, or peers may lead us to believe that we need a new car to be successful, or certain fashions to look good. Many people waste money this way, trying to buy security, a sense of belonging, and self-esteem through possessions. After your basic needs are met, perhaps one of the remaining three areas is a better use of your money.

Services

Many basic services are necessities, like electricity, trash pickup, and auto repair. But people sometimes buy services when they could do the same work themselves with a little training or effort. Or, they buy services that aren't really necessary, like the extra service found at an expensive restaurant, having washable clothes dry-cleaned, or having fingernails done at a salon. When this happens, the person is often attempting to buy something other than the service itself. Could it be that what they actually want is an experience?

Experiences

Money also can provide experiences, such as vacations in exotic lands, tasting new foods, or visiting old friends. Done properly, this is a healthy use of money. But there can be a downside. People may overpay when looking for an experience, or the experience may not turn out as desired. You've probably heard stories from people who have taken expensive vacations only to be disappointed. Buying an experience can be a risky venture, as there is no guarantee it will turn out as planned.

So, why not limit or eliminate the cost and go straight for the experience itself? Here's a true story that offers a great example: P.T. wanted to sail around the world for a year. It was an impossibly expensive dream, requiring both a boat and a crew, yet P.T. realized her dream. She trained as a crew member, then walked along the boat slips in Los Angeles until she found a family embarking on a world trip. After interviewing with the family, she signed on as a crew member. P.T. recognized that she didn't really want a boat or a crew. She wanted an experience, so she found a way to get it without money. Perhaps you can do the same with your dreams!

Feelings

Isn't this often what people are really trying to buy when they buy possessions and experiences? A feeling of belonging. Of being loved. Feeling good about oneself. This is perhaps the most common use of money, but feelings cannot be bought directly. Instead, people buy possessions or experiences in the hope that they will provide these feelings.

Sometimes it works, and money helps make those good feelings happen. Being able to travel to Grandmother's for Thanksgiving, or to fly to the wedding of your best friend, is what makes memories. But often, because our goals aren't clear or we misdirect our resources, we may find ourselves with only the feeling of having nothing to show for our hard-earned money.

Go for the Goal

Refer back to the Life's Accomplishments worksheet on page 15. Think about what you would like to accomplish with the added perspective of what you've just learned regarding the four things money can buy. Then ask yourself the following questions to really focus on achieving those goals. (Note: Writing down the answers can help you clarify your thoughts and often results in a greater commitment.)

What are my goals and dreams?

Why are they important to me? Are they important to me, or am I working to please somebody else (parents, spouse, neighbors, etc.)?

_____

_____

_____

Are my goals realistic?

If your goal is to end world hunger, you might be disappointed. But, if your goal is to contribute a certain amount of time or money to the cause, you'll probably succeed.

_____

_____

_____

Which goal on my list is most important?

Organize your goals in order of priority.

_____

_____

_____

Do I need more money to achieve the things I want?

If so, what are you going to do to get it? You can change your spending habits (we'll show you how later!), learn about money and investing through reading and courses, or re-evaluate the direction of your career.

_____

_____

_____

Am I willing to pay the price to achieve my goals?

Letting go of less important goals will free up resources for goals that matter most.

_____

_____

_____

Are there less expensive ways to fulfill my dreams?

Many people mistakenly believe more money is the answer when there may be a creative way to achieve a particular financial goal without accumulating more money. A less expensive home can reduce retirement expenses. Sending your child to a community college for the first two years will cut college costs. Also, some goals don't require money. Instead, these goals require that you realign your priorities so you have the time and energy to focus on them. How will you do that? What lesser activities will you eliminate to free up the time to focus on your true goals?

_____

_____

_____

What's my "Plan B"?

If things don't go quite as planned (and we all know that's often the case), what will you do? For example, what if you find you can't retire when you want to? How will you scale back expenses and/or increase savings?

_____

_____

_____

Now that you've mapped out your goals and know what you want your money to do, it's time to learn how to change your spending practices so that you can achieve your dreams. The key point to remember is that attitudes and habits can change — that's what this book is all about. You don't necessarily need a million dollars to accomplish your goals, but rather a million-dollar attitude!

Wealth is the result of habit.

CHAPTER 2

The Seven Spending Personalities

Some years ago, I witnessed a woman lose her entire life savings in less than 48 hours. It all began late one Friday afternoon, when Mrs. M. called for an appointment. At the time, I was a practicing financial planner and Registered Investment Advisor. Mrs. M. had received $180,000 from her late husband's life insurance policy several weeks earlier and had decided it was now time to do something with the money. Since it was so late on Friday, I gave her an appointment on Monday morning. She missed it. When I called to find out why, Mrs. M. told me that a stockbroker called her Saturday afternoon, then stopped by later that day. She had invested her entire life savings with a person she barely knew, based on a phone call!

I was stunned. How could anyone make such an impulsive decision with their life savings? I said, "Mrs. M., you know that the stock markets aren't open on the weekend, don't you?" She said yes, so I went on. "Well, your friends had recommended that you work with me, and you knew that the first appointment was free, right?" Again, she said yes. "Well, I just don't understand why you didn't come in first. You would have gotten a second opinion for free, and your money could still have been invested today."

I can still recall her exact words. "I just couldn't wait. I had to do something," she lamented.

Unfortunately, the stockbroker put all her money into only two investments. One investment was an oil and gas limited partnership. In less than a year, it experienced financial difficulties, and Mrs. M. lost almost all her life savings.

Though Mrs. M.'s mistake was particularly devastating, as a financial planner I'd had the opportunity to see lots of mistakes! Eventually, I found that most people have a particular style of spending that falls into one of seven patterns, called "spending personalities."

The habits reflected in your spending personality can have a tremendous impact on your financial well-being. Yet, because they are habits, very often you may repeat them without being aware of what you're actually doing. However, simply becoming aware of your own spending personality patterns will give you a measure of control over them. After reading the chapters that follow, you'll be more likely to question your expenditures to make sure they're in line with your goals rather than the result of spending habits.

To understand how spending personalities develop, imagine a long chain. Many factors influence our spending habits; some go all the way back to childhood, while others, like advertising, are part of everyday life. Each of these factors is a link in the chain, and each helps build a spending personality.

The final and most critical link is the spending decision itself. It is here that all previous influences come together to affect the outcome. Although the chain takes a lifetime to build, breaking just the final link — the spending personality pattern — is enough to break the chain and prevent a mistake from occurring.

Most people have a dominant spending personality — a pattern they follow more often than the other six. When you learn your dominant style, you can concentrate most of your efforts on controlling or eliminating that pattern.

If you find you have traits of more than one personality (and many people do), don't worry. You will learn steps to overcome each in the following pages. It's important to also realize that the emotions surrounding your purchases can determine which spending tendencies you follow. For example, perhaps you find buying clothes enjoyable but buying a new car is a real hassle. In this case, your personality might change from an Impulsive Spender (one who buys clothes on a whim) to a Passive Spender (one who procrastinates buying a car).

Understanding the seven spending personalities also makes it easier to communicate with others (including your spouse and children) about money. Although money is one of the most frequently cited causes of family arguments, some psychologists believe that the problem isn't money itself, but conflicting values and attitudes about money. These conflicts can be resolved more easily when couples know each other's spending personality and understand why their partner spends the way he or she does.

As you read the spending personality chapters, think about recent spending decisions you've made (whether large or small), and how you made them. Did they contribute to the goals you identified earlier? How would things be different if you'd made another decision? You'll soon realize that understanding *why* you make the decisions gives you the power to change.

*If your outgo exceeds your income,
then your upkeep will be your downfall.*

World War II poster

CHAPTER 3

Impulsive Spenders

Impulsive Spenders form the largest personality group. Surveys in my workshops indicate that 41 percent of participants identify this as their dominant spending personality. You've probably experienced impulsive buying yourself. How often have you returned from a shopping trip to find that you've spent more than you planned, or bought an item you had no thought of buying when you left home?

For most people, this is only a minor problem, but you'd be surprised how those little mistakes can add up! Impulsive Spenders buy items they don't need and can't afford. These people struggle to achieve their financial dreams because little "must haves" eat away at any savings they accumulate.

What causes impulsive spending? One factor is lack of clear financial priorities. When faced with an unneeded purchase, Impulsive Spenders can't think of anything else they want more at the time. Without a good reason *not* to spend the money, it's easy to make this common money mistake.

Like any other personality trait, impulsive spending can exist in varying degrees. Some people exhibit it occasionally, but for others, the need for immediate gratification can overwhelm other priorities and create financial problems.

The following test will show you whether impulsive spending tendencies are costing you money.

Are You an Impulsive Spender?

1 — Never   2 — Seldom   3 — Once in a while   4 — Frequently   5 — Almost always

Do you make unplanned purchases when shopping?
    1   2   3   4   5

Do you buy things just because they are on sale?
    1   2   3   4   5

Do you buy items you don't really need?
    1   2   3   4   5

Do you buy items worth more than $100 without comparison shopping?
    1   2   3   4   5

Do you get frustrated when you see something you want and you can't buy it?
    1   2   3   4   5

Do you enjoy shopping?
    1   2   3   4   5

The more answers to the right of the scale, the greater your tendency toward impulsive spending.

Conquer the Impulses

For many people, impulsive spending may be nothing more than a lack of clear priorities or money skills, or an occasional lapse in self-discipline. Still, I've found it to be the number-one spending mistake. If you have impulsive spending tendencies, here's how to conquer them.

Leave the physical presence of the item.
It's the old "out of sight, out of mind" trick. The urge to buy is most powerful while looking at the possible purchase. Once a shopper leaves the presence of the item to "think about it," he or she usually will not return!

Practice the Rule of Three.

Compare prices in three locations. Comparison shopping is especially important if you're an Impulsive Spender, since it forces you to leave the presence of the item. It also makes you think about whether the item is worth investing the time and energy in comparison shopping.

Follow the Empowered Spender Checklist.

Using a checklist requires logic. Since impulsive spending is an emotional decision, this one step can virtually eliminate it. In Chapter 11, you'll learn to use the Empowered Spender Checklist to prevent all seven spending mistakes.

Avoid impulsive-spending locations, like malls and department stores.

This is only a temporary crutch while you're building new, positive spending habits. You'll soon be able to return to these places with a new spending philosophy.

Carry only enough money to make planned purchases.

Avoid carrying credit cards and ATM cards until you've gained control of your spending habits. Since credit cards can make it easier for us to spend impulsively, here are five tricks to stop the charging:

1. **Freeze your credit cards** in a bowl of water. By the time you defrost them, it's likely the urge to charge will have passed.

2. **Lock credit cards in your safe deposit box** and give the key to a trusted relative or friend.

3. **Cancel all credit cards except one.** Keep that one card at home instead of in your wallet.

4. **Get an extra checkbook ledger.** Every time you charge something, record it in the extra ledger (your credit card ledger), just as if you wrote a check. Then take the balance from your credit card ledger and subtract it from the balance in your checkbook ledger to see how much money you really have available.

5. **Volunteer at your local consumer credit counseling center.** You'll reap the rewards of helping others and probably be motivated to get out of debt yourself!

Put the item on layaway if you simply must have it.

Later, when calmer thinking returns, you can cancel the purchase if you change your mind. (Be sure to check the store's layaway policy. There is usually a three- to five-dollar fee to do the layaway paperwork, and there may be a cancellation charge.)

Make a list of desired purchases.

Place it on your refrigerator door. Avoid making the purchases for one to three months. This gives you a specific reason to save, and it helps you re-evaluate desires versus needs.

Spend by choice.

Don't look at the spending decision as a choice between having something or missing out. Instead, go for the goal! See it as a choice between having something minor now or something you really want in the future. That way, avoiding the impulsive purchase isn't denial, it's merely delayed gratification! Spending by choice is one of the key steps on the Empowered Spender Checklist. You'll learn more about that later.

A study of economics usually shows that the best time to buy anything is last year.

Marty Allen

CHAPTER 4

Fanatical Spenders

A lmost everyone knows a Fanatical Spender. They are the people who will drive across town to save a few pennies! Instead of buying immediately like Impulsive Spenders, these folks search for weeks to find the lowest price. They expend excessive time and energy to save comparatively small amounts of money. Again, it's a good intention carried to an extreme.

Fanatical Spenders see spending decisions as a win/lose battle. It's not the item that drives the purchase, but rather their need to control money. As a result, some Fanatical Spenders will fume for days when they find a recently purchased item on sale for a few dollars less.

Fanatical Spenders may not save money in the long run because they may neglect quality in their quest for the lowest price. They may even get so carried away they buy an item they don't need just because it has a super discount! Curiously, Fanatical Spenders can get so obsessed with finding discounts that they buy a more expensive item because it has a higher discount. Apparently, they rationalize they are saving even more money!

Fanatical spending is easy to identify because the characteristics are so different from the other spending personalities. This test can help you determine if you have fanatical spending tendencies.

Are You a Fanatical Spender?

1 — Never   2 — Seldom   3 — Once in a while   4 — Frequently   5 — Almost always

Would others consider the time you spend shopping for bargains excessive?

   1   2   3   4   5

When you buy at the lowest price, are you later disappointed with the item's quality?

   1   2   3   4   5

When you buy at the lowest price, do you later find the item doesn't have all the features you needed?

   1   2   3   4   5

Does it upset you if an item goes on sale shortly after you purchase it?

   1   2   3   4   5

Do you shop for weeks for the best price?

   1   2   3   4   5

The more answers to the right of the scale, the greater your tendency toward fanatical spending.

Keep Perspective

Fanatical spending is relatively easy to correct, since most Fanatical Spenders know the basics of smart shopping. They also learn quickly because of their strong desire to save money. What the Fanatical Spender needs is a balanced perspective. Here's how to build it.

Make it a game instead of a war.

There really is a battle to control your money, since advertisers spend billions of dollars to influence your buying decisions. Instead of seeing it as a war, approach it as a game. To win, you must achieve your overall goals, not win every single battle. So, don't be overly concerned about one purchase.

Value your time and energy.
Saving a few dollars is nice, but is it really worth the time and energy spent? Put a dollar value on your time so you don't spend $50 worth of time to save $5.

Be human.
Fanatical Spenders tend to ignore their successes. Instead of fuming over $10 of missed savings, think of the money you *have* saved. If you feel you made a mistake, allow a short time to be upset, but then learn from it and get on with life. It isn't healthy to expend $100 worth of stress over $10 in lost savings!

Consider needs and value.
A few dollars saved isn't worth the ultimate price if the product does not meet your needs or breaks soon after purchase.

*The fine print in a contract often proves
educational — whether you read it or not.*

CHAPTER 5

Passive Spenders

When it comes to buying, Passive Spenders are just that — passive. They often dislike shopping, frequently procrastinate until the eventual purchase costs more, don't comparison-shop, and seldom ask questions. Some Passive Spenders are just too busy to shop wisely, while others place a low priority on saving money. However, the biggest problem for Passive Spenders is their tendency to get talked into buying items they don't need or can't afford.

One reason Passive Spenders don't ask questions is that they don't want to be embarrassed by their lack of knowledge about a product. This can happen even to people who are very confident in other areas of their lives — a successful executive who has to shop for a new car, for example. Because they may lack expertise in that area, Passive Spenders may feel uncomfortable confronting a salesperson with questions. As a result, some have low sales resistance and allow themselves to get talked into purchases.

In effect, some Passive Spenders let the salesperson make the decision for them. They can then disavow any responsibility for making it. They seldom accept responsibility for their own actions if the purchase doesn't turn out as expected.

Are You a Passive Spender?

1 — Never   2 — Seldom   3 — Once in a while   4 — Frequently   5 — Almost always

Do you avoid comparison shopping?
    1   2   3   4   5

Do you put off making a needed purchase?
    1   2   3   4   5

Are you reluctant to ask questions when shopping?
    1   2   3   4   5

Do you have little sales resistance?
    1   2   3   4   5

Are you dissatisfied with purchases?
    1   2   3   4   5

Do you dislike shopping?
    1   2   3   4   5

The more answers to the right of the scale, the greater your tendency toward passive spending.

To Control Passive Spending

Unfamiliar situations
Ask questions! It's impossible to be an expert on every purchase, so don't be embarrassed by a lack of knowledge. Go to the library or visit Internet Web sites to research an item you intend to purchase. This will help you understand what to look for and provide ideas about questions to ask. Remember, you're spending *your* hard-earned money. Nobody has more of an interest in this than you do.

Intimidation
More people are intimidated by salespeople than are willing to admit it! Remind yourself that you control the spending decision.

Too busy

If you feel you're too busy to spend time shopping wisely, stop and think why it is you are working so hard in the first place. Isn't money necessary to reach one or more of your goals? Why not take a few extra minutes to organize your priorities? Then you can ask the right questions, either to a salesperson or yourself, to ensure that you make the best use of your money.

Procrastination

When the cause of your passive spending is procrastination, try this: Draw a line down the middle of a sheet of paper and list the advantages of acting on one side and the advantages of waiting on the other. The longer list usually points out what you should do.

Time is better spent trying to solve problems than going around them.

CHAPTER 6

Avoidance Spenders

Whoever said, "When the going gets tough, the tough go shopping," certainly described the Avoidance Spender. Shopping is a quick fix for stress, since buying something nice can make us feel better and forget our problems. Unfortunately, it's only temporary and can actually compound the original problem. The result: Avoidance Spenders often create financial difficulties in addition to their original stressor!

Avoidance spending results from the "fight or flight" syndrome. When faced with a conflict, we can either stand and fight or run away. Avoiding problems by shopping (or any other means) only makes the original problem worse.

There are three subcategories of avoidance spending: power spending, revenge spending, and affection spending. In each, the buyer avoids the underlying stressor. These are easier to identify than basic avoidance spending because the buyer is usually aware of the reason for the purchase.

Power spending

Power Spenders have a need to control others and use money to demonstrate their power and feel superior. Making a purchase just to show "who is boss" not only damages their finances, but also hurts another person.

Revenge spending

Unlike Power Spenders, Revenge Spenders are usually helpless to control the actions of others. Out of frustration, they spend for revenge. A forgotten birthday or anniversary, for example, may lead one spouse to retaliate by spending money. Money provides a way to get back at the other person.

Affection spending

The Affection Spender attempts to buy love with money. Affection spending may spring from guilt over past actions, an inability to express affection, or a desire to gain the attention of someone special. (Note: Don't confuse showing affection with affection spending. It's certainly OK to occasionally buy your loved ones nice items.)

Are You an Avoidance Spender?

1 — Never	2 — Seldom	3 — Once in a while	4 — Frequently	5 — Almost always

Do you shop to reduce stress?
| 1 | 2 | 3 | 4 | 5 |

Do you find yourself spending money without planning to do so?
| 1 | 2 | 3 | 4 | 5 |

Do you think shopping provides an "escape" from the pressures of life?
| 1 | 2 | 3 | 4 | 5 |

Do you spend money to "get back" at someone?
| 1 | 2 | 3 | 4 | 5 |

Do you buy gifts because you have difficulty showing affection?
| 1 | 2 | 3 | 4 | 5 |

Do you spend money out of guilt?
| 1 | 2 | 3 | 4 | 5 |

The more answers to the right of the scale, the greater your tendency toward avoidance spending.

The Solution

Whether it's just plain avoidance spending or power, revenge, or affection spending, the steps to eliminate it are the same.

Face the underlying stress.

For many Avoidance Spenders, just becoming aware of — and facing — the problem resolves most of it. If not, chances are professional intervention will help. Start with a credit counselor if the problem primarily involves money. If difficulties involve other areas, see an appropriate therapist or other professional. These problems only get worse if allowed to go unchecked.

Use the Empowered Spender Checklist.

One of the best ways to replace emotion with logic is to use a checklist. If you use the Empowered Spender Checklist found in Chapter 11, you can almost certainly eliminate avoidance spending.

Substitute positive coping behaviors.

There will always be stress in our lives. Learning to cope with it in a positive manner can benefit more than just your finances. It can influence your overall health and outlook on life. The best coping mechanisms involve mind and body in a healthy activity. Instead of shopping, play ball with your children. Exercise and sports are also good coping strategies.

I'd rather be laughing on a bicycle than crying in a limousine.

CHAPTER 7

Esteem Spenders

E steem Spenders make spending decisions based on what others will think of them. Esteem spending is prevalent among teens, who simply *must* have the latest jeans or sneakers. These purchases help teens feel they belong to their peer group. For adults, expensive possessions serve as a visible sign of success. In both cases, buyers feel good, but only for a short time. More purchases must be made to continue feeling good.

According to Dr. David Kentsmith, a clinical psychologist, we are socialized to imitate the behavior of others. These imitative behaviors may create financial problems when we can't afford the lifestyles of our role models. For example, if peers drive luxury cars and wear designer clothes, Esteem Spenders must have them also. It doesn't matter if the peers they're imitating are deeply in debt or are Esteem Spenders themselves.

In their fascinating study of American millionaires, *The Millionaire Next Door*, authors Thomas J. Stanley and William D. Danko use three words to describe the truly wealthy: "frugal, frugal, frugal." Although many people judge the financial status of others by their choice of clothes, cars, homes, jewelry, etc., Stanley and Danko found those who are truly well-to-do did not choose an expensive lifestyle. For example, more than 50 percent paid less than $400 for the most expensive suit they ever bought (and one in 10 actually paid $195 or less for their most expensive suit). More than one-third of millionaires tend to buy used cars, and typically spend less than 1 percent of their net worth on the car. In comparison, the average American spends at least 30 percent of his or her net worth on a vehicle.

In general, the authors point out, those who are millionaires achieved that status by choosing to live *below* their means. "Allocating time and money in the pursuit of looking superior often has a predictable outcome: inferior economic achievement," say Stanley and Danko.

True self-esteem is not dependent upon material possessions. It is a feeling of being in control of your life and having value as a person. Taking charge of personal finances is a far better way than esteem spending to feel good about yourself. It's less expensive, too!

Some people are confused by the differences between esteem spending, buying quality, and buying luxuries. Analyze the following statements to help clarify the differences.

"You can't go wrong buying quality."
The more expensive item is not always the best quality and is seldom the best buy. Browse through back issues of any consumer magazine to prove this to yourself. Avoid using this old saying to rationalize wasteful esteem spending.

"Feeling good is worth the money."
Spending money is a short-term, good-feeling "fix." Esteem Spenders can find other, more permanent ways to feel good about themselves. One way to build self-esteem is by taking control of financial decisions.

"All luxuries are esteem spending."
A more positive attitude is to view luxuries as rewards. They should be enjoyed, but they should also be earned. An occasional luxury won't ruin your budget. You'll appreciate it more for having earned it.

Are You an Esteem Spender?

1 — Never	2 — Seldom	3 — Once in a while	4 — Frequently	5 — Almost always

Do you shop in prestigious stores?

1	2	3	4	5

Do you shop for certain brands or labels?

1	2	3	4	5

Do you avoid shopping at discount stores?

1	2	3	4	5

Do you buy items because others have them?

1	2	3	4	5

Does impressing others affect your spending decision?

1	2	3	4	5

Does buying expensive items make you feel good?

1	2	3	4	5

The more answers to the right of the scale, the greater your tendency toward esteem spending.

Conquering Esteem Spending

To conquer esteem spending, ask yourself the following questions. They overlap somewhat with the Empowered Spender Checklist in Chapter 11, but it's better to ask a question two different ways and get the right answer than to ask it once and rationalize the wrong answer!

What will I really lose if I don't buy the item?

Prestige? Good feeling? If it is a feeling, remember to make a spending choice, not a denial. (Note: Spending by choice is the second step of the Empowered Spender Checklist.)

Can an existing or less expensive item meet the same need?

Will my purchase create family or financial problems?

What specific purchase would I be willing to drop from my budget for this item?

Don't rationalize that you can find the money somewhere. Identify a specific purchase that you are willing to give up.

That man is richest whose pleasures are the cheapest.

Henry David Thoreau

CHAPTER 8

Overdone Spenders

An Overdone Spender is one who spends money on a habit, hobby, or other activity to the point that it wastes limited financial resources or causes relationship problems.

Of course, "overdone" can be a relative term. What may appear to be overdone spending to one person may seem perfectly appropriate to another. Still, it's an area that warrants careful scrutiny. It could be your spending is not in keeping with your overall financial goals. In other words, what began as a simple habit or hobby could be misdirecting dollars that would be better spent elsewhere.

It's easy to have a habit grow into a pretty significant expense without realizing it. Review your regular routine for spending patterns. Do you buy a cappuccino every day? Do you dine out once or twice a week? Do you play golf (or the state lottery) every weekend? These behaviors aren't necessarily right or wrong, but you may not realize their real financial impact.

Try calculating the *annual* cost of each of your habits. Often, the daily or weekly amount spent may seem comparatively small, but when viewed over a month or a year, the total expense may surprise you. For example, the typical American family spent an average of $679 per person for restaurant meals in 1994, according to the National Restaurant Association's analysis of the Bureau of Labor Statistics' "Consumer Expenditure Survey." Cutting that amount even by half could provide enough money for a family vacation or a nice contribution to a college fund or retirement plan.

Overdone spending can occur on virtually anything. Take a walk through your home to see if you have more of a particular item than most people would have. It could be figurines, dolls, compact discs, books, magazines, or even types of clothing (e.g., shoes). Once again, consider the total cost. Could the money be better spent elsewhere?

Are You an Overdone Spender?

1 — Never   2 — Seldom   3 — Once in a while   4 — Frequently   5 — Almost always

Do you spend more for a hobby or activity than other people you know?

| 1 | 2 | 3 | 4 | 5 |

Do others consider your hobby or activity excessive?

| 1 | 2 | 3 | 4 | 5 |

Does spending on your hobby or activity force you to scrimp on other necessary spending?

| 1 | 2 | 3 | 4 | 5 |

Does spending on your hobby or activity cause problems in your relationships with others?

| 1 | 2 | 3 | 4 | 5 |

The more answers to the right of the scale, the greater your tendency toward overdone spending.

How Not to Overdo It

Recognize and admit the problem.
As with the other spending habits, recognizing the problem is the first step. Be honest with yourself when deciding whether what started as an innocent hobby or collection has grown to excessive proportions.

Avoid triggers.
If you find collectibles at auctions or garage sales, go to fewer of them. If you have a penchant for shoes, stay out of the shoe stores.

Replace overdone habits with more positive ones.
Eliminating a habit can leave a void that must be filled. Redirect your time and energy to family activities, athletics, or hobbies (as long as they aren't pursued excessively, of course!).

*Worry is the interest paid on trouble
before it starts.*

CHAPTER 9

Hot Potato Spenders

Hot potato spending involves a cycle of procrastination and worry followed by impulsive action (like the juggling of a hot potato). It is one of the most dangerous of all the spending personalities, even though it occurs relatively infrequently.

Hot potato spending typically takes place when someone is faced with a significant, but unfamiliar, financial decision, such as buying a new car or home, or investing the proceeds of a life insurance policy or an early retirement distribution.

Stage one, the procrastination stage, can last weeks or months, and is often preceded by an emotional event leading to the need to make an unfamiliar financial decision. It could be the loss of a spouse through death or divorce. It could be the stress of an upcoming retirement. In some cases (selling a home, for instance), the spending decision itself triggers emotion.

Unable to decide what to do, the Hot Potato Spender puts off the decision for days or even months. As time passes, the worry over making the decision increases. It's as if the fear of making a mistake is so great that the individual is paralyzed into inaction. Finally, like the straw that breaks the camel's back, the pressure becomes too great. The individual must do something, even if it's wrong. *The pressure of making a decision becomes greater than the consequences of making the wrong decision.*

Stage two is usually very sudden. In an emotional state of mind, the Hot Potato Spender is highly susceptible to any sales pitch. The individual may buy impulsively from the very next store or salesperson he or she encounters. Even trusted family advisers can be left out of the decision-making process.

Obviously, when hot potato spending involves large amounts of money, the results can be catastrophic. You may recall the story of Mrs. M. earlier in this book.

It is not necessary for stage one to be preceded by a traumatic event. Sometimes the decision is so complex that it creates the worry. Buying a home is a good example. After considering prices, room sizes, yards, and all the other variables, one couple became so overwhelmed they ignored their original objective: to live in an area with open spaces around them. Six months after they bought a house, the vacant land behind it was developed into an apartment complex, destroying their privacy and reducing their home's value by 15 percent.

Answer the following questions to see if hot potato spending is a threat to your financial well-being.

Are You a Hot Potato Spender?

1 — Never   2 — Seldom   3 — Once in a while   4 — Frequently   5 — Almost always

Do you worry for weeks over major financial decisions or investments?
1   2   3   4   5

Do you act suddenly after putting off major financial decisions?
1   2   3   4   5

Do major financial decisions make you uncomfortable?
1   2   3   4   5

When faced with a major financial decision, do you set an arbitrary deadline to make it?
1   2   3   4   5

After making a major financial decision, do you feel relieved?
1   2   3   4   5

The more answers to the right of the scale, the greater your tendency toward hot potato spending.

How to Conquer Hot Potato Spending

Though hot potato spending does not occur often, the damage to your finances can take years to overcome. It's a good idea to use the following steps for any large purchase or investment:

Put that potato down!
If a traumatic event, such as retirement or the death of a spouse, has taken place, allow your life to return to a normal routine before acting on a spending decision. Don't rush into major financial commitments. Enlist the aid of trusted family members and friends. Even if no stressful event is involved, avoid setting arbitrary deadlines. Just put the potato down!

While waiting, use the time to educate yourself.
Start by learning the basics about the decision you must make. Take an adult education course. Read books. Ask experts. If the decision is beyond your time and skill, at least learn enough to monitor the experts

you will use. Whatever you do, don't just sit and worry. Using waiting time constructively shortens the wait and improves the quality of the eventual decision.

Use the Empowered Spender Checklist to avoid impulsive decisions.

The Empowered Spender Checklist in Chapter 11 is the best way to ensure that you've carefully thought through the decision.

To acquire wealth is difficult, but to spend it wisely is most difficult of all.

CHAPTER 10

The Self-Assessment

urveys in my financial workshops indicate that the Impulsive Spender is, by far, the most common spending personality. Out of 300 participants, 41 percent identified impulsive spending as their primary spending personality. Here's how all the personalities ranked in terms of frequency:

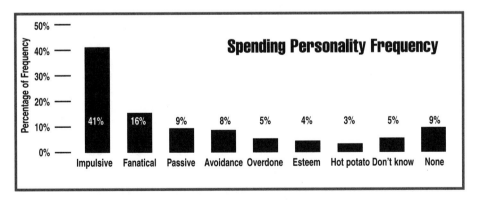

What conclusions can we draw from these numbers? We know the spending personality concept is valid, since almost everyone can identify their primary personality after taking the tests. Of the 5 percent who cannot identify a primary personality, most find two or three personalities for which they have almost equal tendencies, so they can't decide on the primary one. And finally, only one out of every 11 people (9 percent) has no spending personality tendencies.

Most people identify with one personality more strongly than the others, but they also have tendencies in perhaps one or two other areas. The following chart shows how many survey participants, who had already identified their primary personality, also identified a tendency toward at least one other personality.

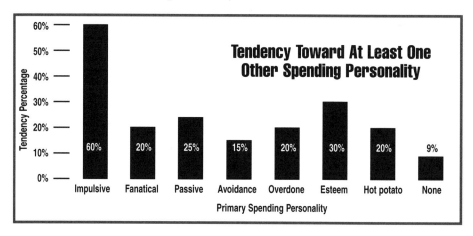

Though not part of their primary spending pattern, these tendencies can still influence spending decisions and need to be controlled. To help you determine your primary personality, as well as any tendencies toward others, please refer to the chapters you just completed and transfer your test answers from each section to the following composite test. This will make it easier for you to see which influences are the strongest.

Spending Personality Assessment

| 1 — Never | 2 — Seldom | 3 — Once in a while | 4 — Frequently | 5 — Almost always |

Impulsive Spender (page 28)

Do you make unplanned purchases when shopping?
  1   2   3   4   5

Do you buy things just because they are on sale?
  1   2   3   4   5

Do you buy items you don't really need?
  1   2   3   4   5

Do you buy items worth more than $100 without comparison shopping?
  1   2   3   4   5

Do you get frustrated when you see something you want and you can't buy it?
  1   2   3   4   5

Do you enjoy shopping?
  1   2   3   4   5

Fanatical Spender (page 34)

Would others consider the time you spend shopping for bargains excessive?
  1   2   3   4   5

When you buy at the lowest price, are you later disappointed with the item's quality?
  1   2   3   4   5

When you buy at the lowest price, do you later find the item doesn't have all the features you needed?
  1   2   3   4   5

Does it upset you if an item goes on sale shortly after you purchase it?
  1   2   3   4   5

Do you shop for weeks for the best price?
  1   2   3   4   5

Spending Personality Assessment (Continued)

Passive Spender (page 38)

Do you avoid comparison shopping?

    1   2   3   4   5

Do you put off making a needed purchase?

    1   2   3   4   5

Are you reluctant to ask questions when shopping?

    1   2   3   4   5

Do you have little sales resistance?

    1   2   3   4   5

Are you dissatisfied with purchases?

    1   2   3   4   5

Do you dislike shopping?

    1   2   3   4   5

Avoidance Spender (page 42)

Do you shop to reduce stress?

    1   2   3   4   5

Do you find yourself spending money without planning to do so?

    1   2   3   4   5

Do you think shopping provides an "escape" from the pressures of life?

    1   2   3   4   5

Do you spend money to "get back" at someone?

    1   2   3   4   5

Do you buy gifts because you have difficulty showing affection?

    1   2   3   4   5

Do you spend money out of guilt?

    1   2   3   4   5

Spending Personality Assessment (Continued)

| 1 — Never | 2 — Seldom | 3 — Once in a while | 4 — Frequently | 5 — Almost always |

Esteem Spender (page 47)

Do you shop in prestigious stores?

   1   2   3   4   5

Do you shop for certain brands or labels?

   1   2   3   4   5

Do you avoid shopping at discount stores?

   1   2   3   4   5

Do you buy items because others have them?

   1   2   3   4   5

Does impressing others affect your spending decision?

   1   2   3   4   5

Does buying expensive items make you feel good?

   1   2   3   4   5

Overdone Spender (page 50)

Do you spend more for a hobby or activity than most other people you know?

   1   2   3   4   5

Do others consider your hobby or activity excessive?

   1   2   3   4   5

Does spending on your hobby or activity force you to scrimp on other necessary spending?

   1   2   3   4   5

Does spending on your hobby or activity cause problems in your relationships with others?

   1   2   3   4   5

1 — Never   2 — Seldom   3 — Once in a while   4 — Frequently   5 — Almost always

Hot Potato Spender   (page 55)

Do you worry for weeks over major financial decisions or investments?
    1   2   3   4   5

Do you act suddenly after putting off major financial decisions?
    1   2   3   4   5

Do major financial decisions make you uncomfortable?
    1   2   3   4   5

When faced with a major financial decision, do you set an arbitrary deadline to make it?
    1   2   3   4   5

After making a major financial decision, do you feel relieved?
    1   2   3   4   5

The personality that has the most answers to the right of the scale is your dominant spending personality. Other categories with answers from "3" to "5" on the scale indicate moderate to significant tendencies toward a particular spending style. All could be costing you money!

Here are four common questions that arise about the spending personalities:

"What if I don't have all the characteristics of any one personality?"

It is not necessary to have all the characteristics of a particular spending personality to fall into that personality category. In fact, it's very common *not* to have them all. If someone fails to ask questions or compare prices, that's a Passive Spender regardless of whether he or she has any of the other traits of passive spending. Don't try to hide your mistakes from yourself by rationalizing, "I only do it once in a while." These are common, everyday behaviors. By increasing your awareness of them, you'll be better able to avoid similar mistakes in the future.

"What is my spending personality? I have characteristics of several."

While many people do have a primary spending personality, some have equal tendencies toward two, three, or even four. If that's you, go back and review the steps for controlling each one. In addition, certain personality traits may surface in particular situations. For example, even though you are not routinely a Hot Potato Spender, those traits may dominate if you are faced with making a major, unexpected financial decision.

"I'm still not sure I know my spending personality. What do I do?"

Chances are that if you suspect you are a particular personality type, you're probably right. If you're really not sure, review all the tests and be certain you've answered the questions as honestly as possible. You might ask your partner or a friend to take the tests for you based on their observations of your spending. This will help ensure you haven't overlooked any blind spots in your spending.

"I don't have any of the spending personality tendencies. What does that mean?"

If you fall into this category, congratulations! Just to be on the safe side, do as suggested above and have someone else answer the questions as he or she thinks they apply to you. After all, we're not always the most objective judge of our own behavior! And do read the rest of this book, because it goes beyond eliminating spending mistakes. It provides money-saving tips you can use immediately, even if you are already doing an above-average job of managing your money.

I have enough money to last the rest of my life... unless I buy something.

CHAPTER 11

The Empowered Spender Checklist

So far, you've learned how to identify your spending personality and avoid its most common mistakes. But avoiding mistakes is only the beginning. It's time to learn to replace old subconscious spending habits with positive new ones.

Even if you don't have significant financial problems, you may be wasting substantial amounts of money. Replacing old habits will help maximize the value of each and every dollar you spend. More importantly, you'll be taking control of your money, rather than letting it control you.

In an earlier chapter, you learned how to determine your deeply felt values and set goals so you could apply them to your spending decisions. The question is, how do you apply those abstract ideas to your day-to-day spending decisions?

The answer lies in becoming an Empowered Spender. To find out whether you're an Empowered Spender, take the following test.

Empowered Spender Test

Do you routinely compare prices of items over $100 in at least three locations?
❑ Yes ❑ No

Do you routinely read consumer reviews on major purchases before buying?
❑ Yes ❑ No

Do you routinely ask for discounts, extras, or upcoming sale prices?
❑ Yes ❑ No

Do you understand your spending personality and take steps to control it?
❑ Yes ❑ No

Do you have three to six months' living expenses saved in an emergency fund?
❑ Yes ❑ No

Do you have a college savings plan for your children and/or a tax-deferred savings plan for retirement?
❑ Yes ❑ No

Excluding your home mortgage, are you debt free?
❑ Yes ❑ No

Do you make deposits each month into a savings account, mutual fund, or other investment separate from your checking account?
❑ Yes ❑ No

Count your "yes" responses.

6 to 8 "yes" responses.
Indicates you are an Empowered Spender with a strong desire to maximize the value of every dollar.

3 to 5 "yes" responses.
Indicates average money skills with room for improvement.

0 to 2 "yes" responses.
Indicates below-average money skills (which I'm about to help you change!).

Note: The ability to answer "yes" to these questions is not necessarily a matter of money. It's a matter of attitude.

The Key to Spending Wisely

The Empowered Spender Checklist

Wise spending doesn't depend on crunching a lot of numbers or learning a lot of sophisticated financial planning techniques. Instead, it relies on an easy-to-use, portable system that works for all spending personalities — a checklist.

Having skills and remembering to use them are two entirely different things. The Empowered Spender Checklist provides 14 simple steps to make the best spending choices in virtually any situation. Just copy the checklist and tape it in your checkbook or wallet, so it will be handy when you need it.

You may notice that the checklist steps overlap slightly. This was done on purpose. For example, some people may rationalize a want into a need (Step 1), but when they get to Step 7 they realize they aren't really getting their money's worth in value. These overlaps protect you from rationalizing a mistake in the heat of a buying decision.

The Empowered Spender Checklist

1. Distinguish between needs, wants, and thinkwees.

2. Spend by choice, not by chance.

3. Find the lowest price.

4. Compare prices in three places.

5. Test-drive the product.

6. Consider new versus used.

7. Buy for the right reason.

8. Maximize your dollars.

9. Consider ongoing costs.

10. Pay cash when possible.

11. Look at total price, not payments.

12. Creatively ask, "Is there another way?"

13. Negotiate and ask for extras.

14. Ask whether the purchase is really a need.

Step 1 — Distinguish Between Needs, Wants, and Thinkwees.

Distinguishing between extravagances and basic needs is fairly simple. Problems arise when people rationalize wants into needs. As noted earlier, we call these false needs *"thinkwees"* — items we *think we* need. In reality, virtually everything beyond basic food and shelter is a thinkwee.

A good example is Albert Schweitzer, the famous medical missionary. He had a small, simple wardrobe and kept his clothes for a long time. For instance, he wore the same black necktie for 20 years. When he was told that some men had *dozens* of ties, he asked, "For one neck?" This was a man who knew the difference between a need, a want, and a thinkwee!

Most people would never buy a Mercedes Benz (a want) if they couldn't afford it. They might, however, rationalize buying a new car (a thinkwee) when a used car (a need) would do just as well. You can usually determine whether a planned purchase is a thinkwee by asking these questions:

- **Do I really need this item?** If the answer is no, you can save 100 percent of the purchase price by not buying it.
- **What problems would not having it create?** Often, not having the item isn't a problem at all. If so, you can save your money for something you really need.
- **Do I want it because others have it or would be impressed by it?** If so, that's esteem spending. It's okay to have an occasional luxury, but don't rationalize that you *need* it. And remember, perceived needs expand with income. New thinkwees will always rise up to eat away at income and savings if you're not careful. Do not let advertising or peer pressure influence your spending.

Step 2 — Spend by Choice, Not Chance.

Many spending mistakes occur because people can't think of anything else that they want more at the time. The problem is that for many people, to buy or not to buy is a *yes/no* decision. You either have something or you have nothing. However, spending by choice is an *either/or* decision. You can either make a self-indulgent purchase now (a superficial gratification), or you can choose to save for an item you really want (a more fulfilling gratification).

Spending by choice ensures that you don't waste money on items that aren't at the top of your needs list. But it takes skill. To help build that

SPEND YOURSELF RICH

skill, plan the purchase of something you desire (it can even be a want or a thinkwee). Let's assume you want a new leather jacket. Visualize how it looks, feels, and smells, and how proud you'll feel knowing you had the discipline to save for it. If you can, tape a picture of it in your checkbook or wallet. Think of it when you are next faced with the prospect of an impulsive purchase. Once you have spent by choice for the jacket (or whatever), switch to another item. After you build your confidence with short-term goals, start including longer-term goals like college or retirement savings.

List the items or goals for which you choose to spend by choice (save for). Then write down why the goal is important. If you wait until faced with an impulsive purchase, you might forget. Once you write down your choice, close your eyes and get a clear image of the item in your mind. Think of how good it will feel to finally reach that goal. Now combine that feeling with the image, so when you think of the item or goal, you automatically feel that same feeling. You will be surprised how powerful this technique can be!

Step 3 — Find the Lowest Price.

How do you know whether a purchase is a bargain if you aren't sure of the lowest possible price? In truth, you really don't know.

Many people make spending mistakes because they think they are buying bargains. If they had taken the time to shop carefully, they probably would find that the so-called bargain price was not a bargain at all. When considering a purchase, ask yourself, "What is the lowest price I have ever seen for a comparable item?" If you are a good comparison shopper, this should give you an idea of the best deal possible. Knowing the lowest price can help you negotiate better bargains and find those one-time good deals.

- **One-time good deals.** There are times to break every rule. The "one-time good deal" could be that time. Let's say you're at a garage sale. You see an item you've wanted for months. The Empowered Spender Checklist requires you to price the item in three places, but if you already know its lowest price, you could consider buying it if the price is good enough. Always remember, however, when something sounds too good to be true, it probably is. Be very careful buying the one-time good deal. Also, be sure to follow the Empowered Spender Checklist to make sure you are not rationalizing an impulsive buying mistake by buying an item you don't really need.

- **The volume advantage.** When you see an item you know you're going to need at or below its lowest known price, you can stock up. Try this with such items as toiletries and office supplies, and you can save up to 75 percent.

- **The negotiating advantage — "I can buy it for less at so-and-so's store."** If you know an item's lowest price, you also have an advantage in negotiating. You can say, "I can buy it at so-and-so's for less," and quote that price. Many sellers will match a competitor's price rather than lose a sale, especially if proper documentation is provided (e.g., a competitor's ad). When you know the lowest price, you have a much better chance of getting it.

Step 4 — Compare Prices in Three Places.

Don't be misled by sales offering discounts. One store's discounted price may be higher than another store's normal price. Only the final price is important, so always compare before buying. As a rule of thumb, compare prices in at least three places (more for higher-priced items and services).

If pricing an item in three places is the only step in the entire book you use faithfully, you will probably save from $400 to more than $1,000 each year, depending on current shopping habits. That might sound high, but a significant part of those savings will come from avoiding impulsive buying mistakes. Comparison shopping forces you to leave the physical presence of the desired item. Remember, most shoppers don't return to buy once they leave the presence of the item.

Here are more tips on comparing prices:

- **Check mail order specialty magazines and liquidators.** It doesn't matter that they are a thousand miles away. Just call and request a catalog. (You can find the toll-free 800 and 888 numbers for any business by dialing 800-555-1212.) Many specialty magazines carry advertisements from discount mail order companies.

- **Check nearby towns.** Expand your horizons.

- **Ask around** to find stores with the best prices. Don't be afraid to ask others for advice.

- **Practice shopping.** Get in the habit of scanning and comparing prices of items you will need in the future. Then you'll know where to find the best prices without wasting time later. If you're a Fanatical Spender, convert some of your energy to "practice shopping." Or, if you're one of

SPEND YOURSELF RICH

the millions who shop just because it's fun, develop the habit of "practice shopping" instead of simply "window shopping."

- **Use the telephone.** Once you know what you want, use the telephone to comparison-shop and save time. You can quickly eliminate merchants with higher prices and those that don't have the item.

Step 5 — Test-Drive the Product.

Would you buy a car without driving it first? Probably not. Yet millions of people don't test products before buying them. This can lead to frustration, disappointment, and wasted money.

Whenever possible, test an item before you purchase it. Of course, direct testing isn't possible with all products, so these tips will help:

- **Consumer reviews.** When it is impractical to test a purchase, the next-best thing is to read the reviews of those who have. Consumer magazines are in your library. In an hour, you can find the results of thousands of hours of testing. Best of all, it's free!

- **Ask around.** Other people's experiences can give a new perspective or prevent overlooking important considerations.

- **Ask about return policies.** Buying a lemon isn't nearly as bad as getting stuck with one! Always ask if the return policy lets you exchange something for a similar item or get your money back.

Step 6 — Consider New Versus Used.

Millions of classified ads, offering everything from household goods to toys and cars, appear daily in newspapers across the country. Often there is little difference between a used and a new item. You can find used items at discounts well below their new prices, so be sure to consider a used item whenever possible.

As a rule of thumb, a used item in good condition is worth about 25 percent of its retail price or 50 percent of its wholesale price. In addition to the classifieds, where and when do you find used items?

- **Local weekly advertising papers** often have many more classified ads than daily newspapers. These are typically available at grocery and convenience stores. Often, they are free.

- **Yard or garage sales.** Concentrate on multifamily sales, and go early for the best selection.

- **Thrift shops and consignment shops** where clothing and other items are sold for a fraction of their original cost.
- **Set up a barter system** among friends, relatives, and neighbors.
- **Off-season.** Check classified ads off-season and at the end of a season for the best deals. When you find a great price on a needed item, act quickly. The early bird gets the worm!

Note on avoiding lemons: Some people sell items that aren't working properly, so be sure to test before buying. Ask about the age of an item and why the owner is selling it. Do the answers sound reasonable? If the seller claims an item is nearly new, ask to see the purchase receipt and/or the owner's manual and warranty information.

Step 7 — Buy for the Right Reason.

Think about what attracts you to a store, hotel, or other establishment. Is it the aesthetics and ambience — the look and feel of the place? Or, is it the value you get when you spend hard-earned money there? If it's the former, you're paying for something you don't really use. Instead, spend your money for the greatest value.

Labels also can be deceptive. Be careful not to buy a product with a famous name (a "label") because you equate it with quality. Quality is important, but it is only one component of value. If you do your homework (comparison shopping, research, etc.), you'll know if that "label" is truly a good value.

Finally, don't get talked into buying an item you don't need and can't afford. Remember, your objective is to save money. You don't have to wear, eat, drive, or own anything, or spend money in any way that doesn't support your goals and values. Take control of your spending decisions. It will improve your life.

Step 8 — Maximize Your Dollars.

Are you getting the maximum amount of happiness, convenience, or experience from every dollar you spend? Could the dollars spent on an item buy more if they were spent elsewhere? If so, don't spend where you aren't getting maximum value for your money.

For example, say you're shopping and notice that a movie you've wanted to see is now available on videocassette. Perhaps, instead of spending $20 to buy the tape, you could rent it for $3 and invite some friends over for the evening to watch it with you. Use the remaining $17 for light refreshments, and you've created an enjoyable evening for yourself and others.

Step 9 — Consider Ongoing Costs.

People often forget to consider the ongoing costs of their purchases, yet these can sometimes be larger than the initial purchase price. There are two types of ongoing costs. The first is related to the normal operation of an item. This might include compact discs for a CD player, monthly service charges for a cellular phone, ink cartridges for a computer printer, or insurance premiums for cars.

The second cost to consider is repairs and maintenance. How often will it break? How much will it cost to repair? How long will it last before it has to be replaced? This is especially important for expensive items like automobiles and computers. Some products (and brands) cost more to repair and maintain. One type of car may not break down often, but when it does, it may cost substantially more than others to repair. You can determine repair histories of products by reading consumer reviews in your library or talking with repair people. Remember, asking questions is healthy.

Step 10 — Pay Cash When Possible.

Buying too much (and the wrong things) on credit is probably the single biggest mistake most people make in their personal finances. Credit can be useful for large purchases and can be safer than carrying large amounts of cash when traveling. But it should be used sparingly, and with thought. Here's why:

- **Payments can make you forget to consider the total cost of an item,** which is often very high. If you use credit, be certain you know the item's total cost, including finance charges and add-ons.

- **Cash has clout.** Cash can give you more negotiating power. It is not unusual to negotiate discounts of 10 to 20 percent on some items.

- **Cash prevents overspending.** When money gets really tight, people paying cash tighten their belts and adjust. Without careful monitoring, credit can let spending get out of control. By the time you recognize the seriousness of the problem, it can already be a financial disaster. According to R. Blue in *The Debt Squeeze*, creditors have found that

THE EMPOWERED SPENDER CHECKLIST

merely putting a credit card in someone's hand will cause them to spend 34 percent more than they would with cash.

- **Cash prevents the "Can we afford it?" oversight.** When buying on credit, too many people wonder only if they can afford the payments *right then.* They forget about expenses that don't occur every month, like back-to-school clothes, birthdays, vacations, insurance premiums, or unexpected emergencies. When these expenses come up, there may not be enough money to cover them as well as the credit payments.

- **Cash eliminates expensive interest.** A typical 36-month loan for merchandise increases its total cost by 25 percent. If you use credit for anything other than very large purchases, make sure you can pay off the balance monthly.

- **Cash reduces spending personality mistakes** like impulsive buying, because there is less money to spend. Buying on credit lets you make mistakes with money you haven't even earned yet!

- **Cash prevents credit abuse.** Financial counselors agree that credit abuse is the number-one reason for personal financial problems. Of course, the true cause is rooted in spending personalities, but easy credit allows these spending personalities to run out of control.

Charge!

The following signs are indications that you should be making *significant* changes in the way you use your credit card(s):

- You pay only the minimum amount due each month.
- You accept *new* credit cards, or increase the credit limit on existing cards, to get access to more funds.
- Your outstanding balance grows even though you make regular payments.
- You lose track of your charges so your monthly statement is a surprise.
- You use your credit cards for everyday purchases (e.g., food, clothing, doctor visits), and don't pay your cards off each month.

Source: National Foundation for Consumer Credit

Step 11 — Look at Total Price, Not Payments.

Although Step 10 recommends paying cash, ours is a "gotta have it now" society. Some people will ignore Step 10 and buy on credit.

However, looking at the total price, not just a monthly payment, gives the credit buyer one more chance to avoid an expensive spending mistake.

Watch for hidden fees and interest. To determine the total cost, simply multiply the monthly payment by the number of months you must make it. Then ask yourself whether you would buy the item if you had to pay that total amount now.

For example, you might get a home demonstration of a deluxe vacuum cleaner with lots of attachments and the ability to suck up bowling balls and small household pets. The cost is only $37.50 per month for three years. Multiplying $37.50 per month by 36 months equals $1,350!

So, don't rationalize those tempting low monthly payments. Always calculate the total cost. *After all, you are going to pay every penny of it eventually.*

Step 12 — Creatively Ask, 'Is There Another Way?'

Is there another way to meet your need? Maybe there is a less expensive way or even one that's free. These ideas often involve using items in ways that were not originally intended. In my home, we converted two antique Greek vases we already owned into table lamps. Our one-of-a-kind lamps are now conversation pieces in our living room, and they were a fraction of the cost of buying new designer lamps.

Using creative ways to save money is a way of life for Amy Dacyczyn, founder and editor of *The Tightwad Gazette* newsletter. "Even relatives who lived through the Great Depression think I'm too thrifty," says this mother of six. When faced with raising a large family on an income of less than $30,000 a year, she chose to make finding ways to save money a personal challenge.

Here are just a couple of Amy's suggestions:

- Use a heaping tablespoon of soy powder and a tablespoon of water as a substitute for eggs in baking. It's healthier and cheaper.

- Make your own fabric softener sheets by pouring a tablespoon of liquid fabric softener onto an old face cloth and popping it into the dryer.

You may think these examples are a bit extreme, but that's exactly the point. We are a nation of "over consumers," throwing away many items that are perfectly useful in another role. If you're the type that enjoys pinching pennies (and you can control any fanatical shopping tendencies!), you can have fun finding creative ways to use items for other than their original purpose. The actual savings on each item may be small, but it adds up. Plus, it's far better to gain a sense of accomplishment from saving money than from spending it!

If you have Internet access, search for "frugal" and you'll find many creative ways to cut costs.

Step 13 — Negotiate and Ask for Extras.

As a buyer, you have as much right to ask for a discount as a seller has to offer it. There's a real sense of pride and accomplishment when you negotiate a discount. One way is to inquire about upcoming or previous sales. If the item was on sale last week, chances are good that you can still buy it at that price if you ask the manager. Just make it clear that you want the sale price or you will leave. When faced with a small profit or no profit, many smart businesses will take the small profit. Also, get in the habit of asking that extras, such as service, supplies, or repairs, be included in the purchase price. Even companies that don't normally discount prices will often provide extras to induce you to buy.

For used items, the price is always negotiable. Often you can get up to 25 percent off, and perhaps even more at flea markets and garage sales, merely by asking. Bargaining and asking for discounts can save you a bundle over the years.

Step 14 — Ask Whether the Purchase Is Really a Need.

The last step in the Empowered Spender Checklist is to ask yourself one final time if the purchase is *really* a need. Sometimes in the excitement of shopping or trying to find the best bargain, we can lose sight of our original objectives. This is common in all the spending personalities, but it probably occurs most frequently among Fanatical Spenders and Impulsive Spenders. They find it hard to pass up a great bargain even though they really don't need the item. Because the discount is greater, they may buy a more expensive item to "save" more money.

Take the case of Jeff, who planned to spend $10,000 for a small pickup truck. While at the dealership, he saw a full-size van — normally $23,000 — on sale for $19,000. It even had a rear-seat television! A smart shopper, Jeff used a buying service to learn the dealer's cost. He drove the van over the weekend to test it. Finally, he negotiated an even better deal, buying the van for about $18,000. What a great bargain ... or was it a spending mistake?

SPEND YOURSELF RICH

Even with the discount, Jeff paid $8,000 more than he had originally planned. Instead of selling his old pickup, he had to keep it because the van couldn't carry what he needed. In the excitement of negotiating a great deal, Jeff lost sight of his original criteria for the purchase.

Using the Checklist

If you haven't done so already, make a copy of the Empowered Spender Checklist. Tape it in your checkbook or wallet. Use it for every purchase for the next two months. It takes only a few seconds. If it takes longer, it could mean you are on the verge of making a spending mistake! If you follow its steps for two months, they will become habits. You'll do them automatically, and just as importantly, you'll be proud of your new money skills! It just might change your life.

*Every parent should remember that one day
their children will follow their example and
not their advice.*

CHAPTER 12

Children and Spending

From the time they're very young, children learn that money is important in our society. They see their parents happy and despondent over it, and hear them argue about it. They know that money (or what it can buy) will often be given to them as a reward for good behavior or performance, or taken away as punishment. It's no wonder that attitudes toward money are formed quite early.

You may not realize it, but how you manage money on a day-to-day basis will affect your children's ability to manage money as an adult. Your financial habits are a role model for your children. Just as we impart to our children our beliefs on everything from religion to eating, we also convey views and habits on spending money. How do you teach good money skills? Here are some tips.

Start early.
You can begin basic money lessons as early as the age of three or four.

Teach smart shopping.
Teach your kids how to comparison-shop, look for sales, and compute markdowns.

Let them make spending mistakes.
Mistakes are one of life's most powerful teachers. Teach and guide your children, but allow them to make their own mistakes. You may know that cheap toy they're buying will fall apart before the day's out, but hopefully, they'll buy smarter the next time. Besides, it's better to make small mistakes as a child than expensive ones as an adult.

Teach older children to balance a checkbook.
You'd be amazed at how many *adults* don't know how to do this.

Let your children help you pay the bills.
This helps them learn just how much it costs to run a household. It also helps them understand why it's necessary to budget and plan for expenses. If your children are young, you can show them the bills and explain what each is for, then let them help by licking stamps and sealing envelopes. Older children can enter amounts into your checkbook register and calculate the balance.

Talk money with them.
Discuss the family budget, tax returns, and investments. Naturally, the information needs to be age-appropriate. Even though young children won't understand taxes (who does?), they can learn that sales tax is an additional amount you have to pay on certain purchases.

Set a good example.
Children take their money cues from their parents. If you earn, spend, and save wisely, your children are more likely to do so as well.

The Allowance Dilemma

Experts agree that giving a child an allowance is a good idea, but how much should it be? What should it cover? When should you increase it?

The amount of an allowance should depend upon the child's age, your budget, and what you expect the allowance to cover. Whatever amount you decide, give it regularly just like a paycheck. Help your child understand that when the allowance is gone, he or she must wait until the next payment. Then don't back down! If your child spends the entire allowance then wants a toy, don't give in and buy the toy. Use it as a teaching opportunity to show your child the necessity of budgeting and planning and to emphasize that we all must set priorities for our spending.

When you begin to give a child an allowance, make the rules very clear. Take extra time to make sure your child understands what is expected and how the allowance is to be used. If you're going to require that a certain amount or percentage must be saved, perhaps you can provide a special jar or bank for that money. Some parents also make certain their children set aside money for their church or charitable purposes, teaching yet another valuable lesson.

You also must be specific about what expenses a child has to cover with his or her allowance. Older children might be responsible for paying for their own clothes, dates, CDs, and entertainment, while younger ones could pay for toys, games, and special treats. Failure to clearly establish the child's responsibility at the outset will result in confusion and attempted manipulation later on. Remember, this is a new area for your child, and you must be careful to explain the rules.

Of course, all good rules have exceptions! Unanticipated situations arise for children just as they do for adults. Be ready to listen and bend your rules for legitimate needs.

And last, but not least, expect mistakes. Offer suggestions, but resist the desire to control how your child spends money. Watch for a pattern of mistakes, not just one (we all make them!). If there is a pattern, does it match one of the spending personalities? A child who continues to make the same type of mistake may need firm, but understanding, supervision. Children who catch on quickly to good money management can be rewarded with more responsibility, such as a savings or checking account.

Learning While Earning

If your children are old enough to work for money, whether baby-sitting or taking on a summer job, you can help them learn while they earn. Encourage them to:

- **Set aside a portion of their earnings.** It's a good idea to open a savings account and have your kids put away an agreed-upon percentage of their earnings. You may also want to encourage them to invest in a mutual fund, matching their investment dollar-for-dollar (or 25 or 50 cents per dollar). Show them how investments rise and fall in value. A 15-year-old who starts contributing $1,000 annually to an individual retirement account (IRA), earning an 8 percent return, could have almost $600,000 by age 65. (This is a hypothetical example for illustrative purposes only. This is not a prediction or guarantee of actual results.)

- **Learn from spending mistakes.** Once again, let your kids know you won't bail them out if they overspend. In a true emergency, when borrowing is necessary, set up a formal repayment plan.

- **Keep a balanced checkbook** and set up a simple record-keeping system for personal expenses. Visit financial institutions together and compare the costs and features of different accounts.

- **Practice the Rule of Three** before spending hard-earned cash. That is, comparison shop in at least three different places for major purchases, such as auto insurance.

*A child thinks twenty shillings and twenty
years can scarce ever be spent.*

Benjamin Franklin

CHAPTER 13

Saving for Children: The Cost of College

A college education is one of the greatest assets your children can have. But it is expensive. To save for a public education, you would have to set aside $150 to $200 a month above your other savings for at least 15 years. Saving that kind of money can seem overwhelming. The key is to get started as soon as possible, and begin with an amount you can comfortably afford.

If your child has more than five years before attending college, you can consider long-term investments, such as a growth-oriented mutual fund,* because you will have time to absorb swings in the market. When a child reaches 16 or 17, you may want to balance the account with a bond fund or certificates of deposit. The year before college, put more of the money into a money market or regular savings account so you can get to it easily.

---

*Please keep in mind that the return and principal value of a mutual fund will fluctuate, so that an investor's shares, when redeemed, may be worth more or less than their original cost.

Series EE Savings Bonds, which are sold by the U.S. government, are another excellent tool. If you buy them in your name and later cash them in for college tuition and fees, the bonds' earnings will be exempt from tax unless your income exceeds certain limits.

If your teenager will be ready for college in a few years and you haven't been able to save much, there are a couple of things to do. First, have your teenager take advantage of advanced placement courses offered at most high schools. These classes give college credit, and in some cases, kids can get the first year of college under their belts before they graduate from high school.

In addition, ask your child's high school guidance counselor for advice on financial aid programs. These individuals have a wealth of information about scholarships, grants, work-study programs, and student loans. Everyone should go through the financial aid application process, even if you think you earn too much. And don't discard the idea of a private college. Often, these schools are better endowed than public institutions and offer generous financial aid packages.

As a last resort, you can take out a loan against your home's equity, an insurance policy, or your 401(k) retirement plan, but be cautious about jeopardizing your own future. And don't forget, kids who work their way through college can end up with a real appreciation of their college education.

Why pay a dollar for a bookmark? Why not just use the dollar as a bookmark?

Fred Stoller

CHAPTER 14

Smart Spending Tips

Once you learn your spending personality and begin applying the steps in the Empowered Spender Checklist, you're well on your way to mastering almost any spending decision that you may face.

This chapter will take you a step further, with practical advice on how to save money on day-to-day expenses.

First, you must know where you're spending your money now. That may sound simple, but few people can account for all of their expenses. To increase your awareness of just where your money goes, try tracking all your expenses (cash, check, and charges) for several months. Use specific categories, including (but not limited to) the following:

- Auto expenses
- Clothing
- Entertainment
- Education
- Gifts
- Groceries
- Household items (furniture, etc.)

- Household expenses (repairs, lawn care, etc.)
- Insurance
- Medical/dental
- Mortgage/rent
- Savings
- Taxes
- Utilities
- Vacations

Personalize the list with any categories of your own. Be sure to include even relatively small expenses, because they often add up to far more than you would expect. For example, a morning cup of coffee at 65 cents per day (five days a week) equals $169 per year. Once you know where the money is going, you can put your new spending skills to work in order to increase the amount of money you can allocate toward your goals. The following tips will also help you cut expenses, even for necessities like food, clothing, and utilities.

Seven Ways to Reduce Debt

If credit card bills and other debts are keeping you from achieving your financial goals, these steps will help you pay off those bills once and for all:

1. **Assess the damage.** Close your eyes and add up in your head the balances on your credit cards and loans. You aren't sure how much you owe? The average person has five or six credit cards with balances totaling more than $2,800, and many people owe a lot more than that. Before you can develop a plan to pay off your bills, you have to figure out how much you owe. Make a list of all your credit cards and loans. Include how much you owe, the required monthly payment, and the interest rate. If you have loans where you don't get a monthly statement, like a car or student loan, call the lender to find out the current balance.

2. **Pay the most expensive one first.** Make only the minimum monthly payment on all your cards except the one with the highest interest rate. Put as much extra money as you can afford each month toward that card until it's paid off. Once you've paid it off, add the same payments you were making on that card to the payments you're making on the card with the next-highest interest rate, and so on.

3. **Just pennies a day.** Marc Eisenson, author of *The Banker's Secret*, has shown hundreds of thousands of people how to pay off their debts early and save a bundle in the process. He points out that by adding just

25 cents a day to the minimum payment on a $1,000 credit card bill with a 17 percent interest rate, you'll save $502 in interest and pay off the bill six years sooner. One trick: Empty your pockets at the end of each day and put the change you find there toward your loan payments.

4. **Out of sight, out of debt.** If you continue to charge on your credit cards, chances are you'll never make headway. Your best strategy is to take your cards out of your wallet, so you won't be tempted to use them. If you must have a credit card for travel or emergencies, choose one that has a zero balance and then resolve to pay any new charges in full when you get the bill.

5. **Bargain-shop.** Suppose you're shopping for tennis shoes. You find the pair you want for $60 at the mall. A discount sporting goods store, however, has the same pair for only $45. Which would you buy? The cheapest pair, of course. The same should be true for your credit cards and loans. The higher the interest rate, the more money that loan is costing you.

Find a card with a low interest rate. For a list of the best low interest rate credit card deals available, call or write to Bankcard Holders of America (BHA), (540) 389-5445, 524 Branch Drive, Salem, VA 24153, and request the "Low Interest Rate List" and "No Annual Fee Credit Card List." The fee is $4. RAM Research also publishes a monthly report listing the lowest interest rate credit cards. The fee is $5. To order, call (800) 344-7714. Credit card interest rate information is also available online from the Bank Rate Monitor's Web site (www.bankrate.com).

Once you've selected a low interest rate credit card, contact the credit card company and tell them you want to use their card to pay off some of your other debts. Most credit card companies will be happy to help you transfer other bills to their cards.

Consolidating credit card bills on a cheaper credit card can save you literally hundreds of dollars while you're paying off the balance. Be sure to cut up the high-rate cards you've paid off. Also, notify the lender to close the line of credit.

6. **Plan for the unexpected.** Jumping off the debt treadmill isn't always easy. Just when you think you're making progress, the car breaks down, or your dentist tells you that your child needs braces — and you don't have the money to pay for it. Expect the unexpected and don't be discouraged if it happens.

7. Reward yourself. Changing your spending habits is hard work. Make a list of things you enjoy that don't cost a lot of money. Reward yourself inexpensively when you pay off a bill or pass up a sale at the mall. The greatest reward, of course, is when your debts are paid and you don't have to worry about bills anymore.

If unexpected expenses are keeping you from paying off your debts, you may want to call a professional for help. A credit counselor can help you develop a spending plan that will work, even when times get tough. Nonprofit consumer credit counseling service agencies offer free budgeting and credit help at more than 1,000 offices nationwide. Call the National Foundation for Consumer Credit at 1-800-388-2227 for the location of the office nearest you.

The Repair or Replace Dilemma

People sometimes use the need for minor repairs to rationalize the unnecessary purchase of a new item. But how do you know when to have an item fixed and when to just replace it? Here's how to make the right decision.

Divide a sheet of paper into two columns. List the reasons to fix the item in one column, and the reasons to replace it in the other. The longer list is usually the best course of action. But be sure your columns answer all the following questions.

- **How much** will replacement cost?
- **Does the old item** have any resale value to offset its replacement cost?
- **How much** will repairs cost?
- **How good** will the item be after repair? Will it be like new, or could another problem soon surface? Ask the repair person about the overall quality of the item.
- **Is the item completely broken,** or can it still perform limited service as it is? For example, a broken clock radio may still have a perfectly good clock. This might offer the opportunity to wait for sales.

Four Ways to Cut Household Expenses

1. Use the 24-hour rule. If you have your eye on an item that costs $100 or more, wait 24 hours before buying it. You'll probably make a smarter decision.

2. **Shop at stores that will refund the difference if an item goes on sale** *after* **you buy it.** Usually, the time limit is up to 30 days after your purchase. Remember to keep your receipt.

3. **Buy from the floor.** Try to buy display models of furniture and appliances — and ask for a discount. Items that require assembly can also be less expensive than their fully assembled counterparts.

4. **Carry less cash and plastic.** Unless you're traveling or making planned purchases, leave your cash, credit cards, and ATM card at home. This will reduce the likelihood of impulse buying.

Trimming Utility Costs

- **Watch your water.** Fixing a leaky faucet could save you up to $300 per year. Other ideas: fix running toilets; use a low-flow shower head; install a programmable timer on your water heater, and decrease your water heater temperature from 140 degrees to 120 degrees.

- **Plug the leaks.** Caulk or weather-strip windows and doors, and install storm windows. Install sweeps at the bottom of doors, and use insulated window treatments, shades, or drapes to block out cold air.

- **Lower your winter temperatures.** For each degree you lower your heat, you'll decrease your heating bill by about 2 percent. Buy a clock thermostat and set it to reduce temperatures at night and when you're away at work. Use a humidifier to increase your comfort at lower temperatures.

- **Cool off air conditioning bills.** Service your air conditioning unit each season. Shade the compressor, allowing room for ventilation. Plant trees and tall shrubs on the west and south sides of the house to provide shade. Close drapes, blinds, or shades when direct sun shines in. Use ceiling fans — moving air feels two to four degrees cooler. Turn off unnecessary lights; 95 percent of the electricity used by light bulbs turns into heat. Use window fans properly. At night when it's cool outside but stuffy inside, open bedroom windows and put a window fan blowing *out* on the opposite side of the house. Keep other windows closed. The fan will draw cool air into your bedroom window.

- **Think efficiency.** Use a microwave or toaster oven for preparing small amounts of food. Turn off lights and appliances when no one is using them. When buying new appliances, check the energy label for energy efficiency and annual operating costs.

- **Plan ahead.** Use dishwashers, dryers, and washing machines at off-peak hours, when utility companies typically charge lower rates. Check with your utility company to see what those hours are.

Taking a Bite Out of Your Food Bill

- **Shop for food no more than once a week.** To avoid impulse buying, shop alone and when you're not hungry. Comparison-shop for nonfood items at discount and drug stores, which often charge less than supermarkets.
- **Set a limit for weekly food purchases.** Shop with a list of items and prices totaled to equal no more than your spending limit. Budget a small amount for unplanned purchases within this amount.
- **Plan menus before shopping** to avoid waste.
- **Nix the snacks.** Avoid buying expensive snack foods and prepare your own instead. Ditto for convenience foods such as single-serving frozen entrees.
- **Look above and below eye level.** The best buys are there.
- **Study unit prices.** If you're buying cereal, for example, don't assume "the large economy size" is the best buy — especially if you're using a coupon. A 75-cent coupon, doubled, could make the smallest size the least expensive.
- **Buy foods in season.** Buying out of season can be very expensive. Change your meals to accommodate seasonal crops or stock up on seasonal produce and can or freeze it.
- **Read back issues of consumer magazines** for reviews on food items. You'll find that the best tasting food isn't always the most expensive.

Dining Out

- **Dine out at lunch.** Most nice restaurants have less expensive luncheon menus.
- **Don't wait until you're starved.** You'll order less if you have a piece of fruit before you go.
- **Consider vegetarian dishes.** They can cost up to 25 percent less and are often healthier.
- **Skip the appetizers.** The typical appetizer adds up to 30 percent to a meal's cost.

- **Avoid alcoholic beverages,** which can increase dining costs by 50 percent! Besides, drinking and driving don't mix.
- **Try cafeterias.** They're less expensive and everyone can eat what they want.

Making Your Wardrobe Dollars Stretch

- **Donate old clothing to charity.** Ask for a receipt and the organization's tax ID number so you can claim a tax deduction. If the clothing is in great shape, take it to a consignment shop that will split the profit with you if they sell it.
- **Shop at outlets.** Manufacturer-owned outlets, found in outlet malls throughout the country, generally offer clothing for less than department and specialty store prices. Ask about upcoming sales.
- **Consider cleaning costs.** Dark coats, jackets, and outerwear will need less frequent cleaning than lighter garments.
- **Accessorize your wardrobe.** Scarves, ties, and jewelry can liven up your wardrobe without costing you a fortune.
- **Handle with care.** Use dishwashing liquid instead of a special detergent for hand-washing delicate garments.

Drive Down Driving Costs

- **Check your owner's manual to determine the fuel octane level you need.** If you buy 93 octane fuel at $1.29 a gallon when you could be using 87 octane at $1.09 a gallon, you're wasting 20 cents a gallon. Multiplied by the 555 gallons the average car owner buys in a year, that's $111.
- **Drive at a constant speed to save fuel.** Fluctuating between 55 and 65 miles per hour in a 65 mph zone, instead of staying at a steady 60 mph, can cost 1 to 1.5 miles per gallon. At 25 miles per gallon and $1.29 a gallon, the potential savings (or loss) is 33.3 gallons, or $45.70 per year.
- **Get a tune-up.** A simple engine tune-up can improve gas mileage by as much as 20 percent. At 25 miles per gallon and $1.29 a gallon, the potential savings is $119.33 per year.
- **Replace your air filter.** A clogged air filter can cost one mile per gallon. Estimated annual savings by replacing it: $29.84.
- **Keep tires properly inflated.** Running tires at improper inflation can steal one mile per gallon. Another $29.84 per year.

- **Make sure your wheels are balanced.** A wheel out of balance by as little as 3 percent can add 36 extra pounds to your vehicle's total weight. Four tires out of balance could equal 144 gas-robbing pounds.

Source: Firestone Tire & Service Centers

How to Save on Car Insurance

- **Multiple policy discounts.** Some auto insurers provide a discount if you purchase both your auto and homeowner's insurance with them. Compare the combined premiums to see if you can save by having one company handle all your coverage.

- **Buy smart.** Insurance companies look at the type of car you drive when they set rates. When you're car hunting, check with your insurance agent to compare premiums on models you like.

- **Increase your deductible.** You might be able to save some serious money by increasing your collision and comprehensive deductibles. If you have a $100 deductible, ask your agent how much you would save by going to $300 or $500.

- **Drop the collision coverage on older cars.** If a car is worth less than $1,000, consider dropping collision coverage. This can be the most expensive part of a policy, and it can make sense to eliminate it on older cars.

- **Shop around.** Getting estimates from multiple insurers can be a nuisance, but do it anyway. You might find some surprising differences in price by comparison shopping.

*Keeping up with the rich is no way
to get rich.*

CHAPTER 15

Set and Keep Your Financial Resolutions

N ow that you've learned how to identify and control your spending personality, and how to save money on everyday expenses, it's time to make some financial resolutions. Lots of people make New Year's resolutions each year, but fail to keep them. Why? Because they set their goals so high that they don't honestly believe they can succeed. As a result, they give up too easily. Here's how to set — and keep — financial resolutions.

- **Don't call them resolutions.** Call them goals or objectives, just like you would at work. It's a subtle difference, but it shows you are taking this seriously.

- **Don't set goals that are too vague or too high.** Be specific and short-term. Goals that are too vague, too high, or too far in the future don't provide enough motivation to save. For example, decide to order a mutual fund application and start monthly deposits for a college education fund as soon as it arrives, rather than simply planning to save for your children's education.

- **Write down your goals.** Studies show that people who write down their goals are less vague and have a greater chance of success.

- **Break your goals down into little steps.** Divide big objectives into smaller, more manageable ones.

- **Set deadlines.** Establishing a timetable helps you focus on your goal.

- **Tell your friends about your goals.** Making a public commitment to friends will help you reach your goals because you don't want to be embarrassed by not following through. That extra conviction can see you through difficult times.

- **Review your goals periodically.** Make a note on your calendar to review your progress 30 to 90 days from now.

Here are a few quick pointers to help keep those financial goals in sight.

- **Don't forget to tape a copy of the Empowered Spender Checklist** in your wallet or checkbook. Remember, knowing good shopping skills and using them are two different things, especially when a new thinkwee beckons. This checklist is a step-by-step way to make the best spending choices in almost any situation.

- **Should you occasionally forget** to apply your newly found spending habits, take a few minutes to determine what you will do differently when a similar situation comes up in the future.

- **Review this book in six months.** If you find you've slipped back into some old spending habits, a quick review should motivate you to return to your new money-saving habits.

- **Lastly, live and spend in harmony with YOUR values and YOUR dreams.** It will give you a sense of focus, inner peace, and fulfillment that mere money can't buy.

References

"Americans & Their Money 10: The 10th National Survey" (1995). *Money* magazine.

Blue, R. *The Debt Squeeze*. Pomona, California: Focus on the Family Publishing, 1989.

Bozell Worldwide. "Quality Quotient Survey," as cited in *Research Alert Yearbook 1995, The Year In Review*. New York: EPM Communications, 1996: 146.

Bureau of Labor Statistics. "Consumer Expenditure Survey." Analysis by the National Restaurant Association as cited in *Research Alert Yearbook 1996, The Year In Review*. New York: EPM Communications, 1997.

Eisenson, Marc. *The Banker's Secret*. New York: Villard Books, 1990.

Miller, Berna. "Fun Money." *American Demographics*, Vol. 19, No. 3, (March 1997): 33.

Stanley, Thomas, Ph.D., and William Danko, Ph.D. *The Millionaire Next Door*. Marietta, Georgia: Longstreet Press, Inc., 1996.

Sullivan, Robert. "Americans and Their Money: An Intimate Portrait." *Worth* (June 1994).

Resources

Budgeting
The Budget Kit by Judy Lawrence. 1997. Dearborn Financial Press. This easy-to-use workbook contains all the forms you need to develop your own budget.

Saving on a Shoestring by Barbara O'Neill, CFP. 1995. Dearborn Financial Press. Loaded with dozens of practical saving tips.

College Education
Federal Student Aid Information, (800) 433-3243. If you have access to the Internet, visit FinAid: The Financial Aid Information Page on the World Wide Web (www.finaid.org).

Financial Aid for College by Pat Ordavensky. 1995. Peterson's. A quick guide to getting available college money, what financial aid officers look for on your forms, and how they award money.

Consumer Information
Consumer Information Catalog. Consumer Information Center, P.O. Box 100, Pueblo, CO, 81002. Many free or low-cost booklets on a wide range of consumer-related topics.

Consumer Resource Handbook by the U.S. Office of Consumer Affairs, Pueblo, CO 81009. A free guide to hundreds of agencies to contact for assistance with consumer-related problems.

Credit
National Foundation for Consumer Credit, (800) 388-2227.

The Ultimate Credit Handbook by Gerri Detweiler. Revised edition, 1997. The Penguin Group. This book is designed to help you take command of your credit. It will show you how to save money on credit, get out of debt, solve your credit problems, and get credit when you need it.

Financial Planning
The Richest Man in Babylon by George S. Clason. Hawthorn/Dutton. This book has been in print since 1926, a testimonial to its timeless message. Easy to read and inspirational.

About the Author

Called "the father of financial wellness," Grady Cash is a former financial planner. He has held licenses as a stockbroker, insurance agent, stockbroker supervisor, Registered Investment Advisor, and has been a Certified Financial Planner® since 1983. At one point, he designed and developed all the financial plans for a prestigious financial services company in Dallas, Texas. A former behavioral counselor, Grady also has several years' experience as a counselor and director of an outpatient substance abuse clinic.

Since developing his values-based approach to personal finance, Grady now delivers keynote speeches and workshops on motivation, personal finance, and other quality-of-life topics to associations and corporate employees. His financial workshops contain no math. Instead, these workshops are focused on overcoming self-limiting beliefs and attitudes toward life and money. This innovative approach has been well-received; for as this is written, Grady remains the first and only financial speaker to address both the National Wellness Conference and the Association for Worksite Health Promotion — the nation's two largest wellness conferences.

Grady is on the Board of Advisors of the National Center for Financial Education and is also active in several financial and health associations. He has been quoted widely and is the author of three personal finance books.

An avid runner, Grady has completed the Athens Marathon in Athens, Greece.

Order Form

FAX:
(616) 552-4320

Call toll-free
1-888-679-3300
Have your credit card ready.
Visa, MasterCard and
American Express accepted.

Mail to:
Financial Literacy Center
350 East Michigan Avenue • Suite 301
Kalamazoo, MI 49007-3851

Name: _____

Street Address: _____

City: _____ State: _____ Zip: _____

Telephone: (_____) _____ Fax: (_____) _____

Pricing:

Quantity	Price Each
1	$14.95+
2 – 10	10.95*
11 – 25	8.95
26 – 50	7.95
51 – 100	6.45
101 – 500	4.95
501+	Call for quote

Please send me the following:
Spend Yourself Rich!
Quantity: _____
ISBN-0-9659638-2-9

Shipping:

+ For 1 book, there is a $2.50 charge for shipping and handling in the 48 continental United States, plus Alaska and Hawaii. For all other countries, we charge $2.50, plus actual postage charges.

* For 2 or more books, there is a 7% charge on the total amount for orders within the 48 continental United States ($7 minimum). For Alaska and Hawaii, and for all other countries, we charge actual postage plus $7. (Please call for a quote.)

Michigan residents please add 6% sales tax.

Payment:
☐ I have enclosed a check.

☐ Credit Card: ☐ **VISA** ☐ **MasterCard** ☐ **American Express**

Card number: _____

Cardholder's signature: _____ Exp. date ___/___/___

Call toll-free and order now!
1-888-679-3300

Order Form

FAX:
(616) 552-4320

Call toll-free
1-888-679-3300
Have your credit card ready.
Visa, MasterCard and
American Express accepted.

Mail to:
Financial Literacy Center
350 East Michigan Avenue • Suite 301
Kalamazoo, MI 49007-3851

Name: _____

Street Address: _____

City: _____ State: _____ Zip: _____

Telephone: (_____) _____ Fax: (_____) _____

Pricing:

Quantity	Price Each
1	$14.95+
2 – 10	10.95*
11 – 25	8.95
26 – 50	7.95
51 – 100	6.45
101 – 500	4.95
501+	Call for quote

Please send me the following:
Spend Yourself Rich!
Quantity: _____
ISBN-0-9659638-2-9

Shipping:

+ For 1 book, there is a $2.50 charge for shipping and handling in the 48 continental United States, plus Alaska and Hawaii. For all other countries, we charge $2.50, plus actual postage charges.

* For 2 or more books, there is a 7% charge on the total amount for orders within the 48 continental United States ($7 minimum). For Alaska and Hawaii, and for all other countries, we charge actual postage plus $7. (Please call for a quote.)

Michigan residents please add 6% sales tax.

Payment:

☐ I have enclosed a check.

☐ Credit Card: ☐ **VISA** ☐ **MasterCard** ☐ **AMERICAN EXPRESS**

Card number: _____

Cardholder's signature: _____ Exp. date ___/___/___

Call toll-free and order now!
1-888-679-3300